Lady Rose Hickman - Her Life and Family

To Di
Very Best Wishes
Sue Allan

By
Sue Allan

domtom publishing ltd

ISBN 978-1-906070-10-6

First published 2009 by domtom publishing ltd

Acknowledgements

The author would like to acknowledge:
her collaborator and researcher,
Roger Thomas Vorhauer together with
Russell Hocking for his contribution to editing.

Printed and bound in the UK by
DPS Partnership Ltd
www.dpsltd.net

Lady Rose Hickman
(1526 - 1613)

Portrait of Lady Rose Hickman -Gainsborough Old Hall.

Portrait of unknown lady thought to be Lady Rose Hickman – private collection.

Lady Rose Hickman – Her Life and Family

Lady Rose Hickman lived at Gainsborough Old Hall from 1596 until her death in 1613. In 1610, at the age of eighty- four, Rose wrote an account of some of the events in her life[1]. She was born Rose Locke, in the City of London on December 27th[2] 1526. During her lifetime, she lived through the reigns of two Tudor kings and nine Tudor queens and into that of King James Stuart.

Rose's father was a fabulously rich Mercer[3] named William Locke. The Lockes were a noble family whose ancestors are thought to include such notables as Leofric Earl of Mercia and his wife, Lady Godiva. Rose was the daughter of William and his second wife, Katherine Cook and was one of twenty children sired by her father in total. William married Katherine in 1524, and had nine children with her – four died in childhood. His first wife, Alice Spence, died in 1522.

Mercers usually dealt in the trading of exports of English cloth overseas and the importation of silk and luxury items for the rich and noble at court. However, William would also procure from abroad whatever the King desired (including quail's eggs to satisfy the cravings Henry's pregnant third wife, Jayne). While abroad, Mercers also often acted as 'the eyes and ears' of the monarch picking up useful intelligence in times of unrest.

Like many other Mercers, William Locke and his family were among a growing number of converts to Continental Protestantism, something regarded in still Catholic England and beyond as *heresy* and punishable by death. Even more dangerous than this, William was involved in smuggling illegal English translations of the Bible and Gospels into England.

Rose writes in her memoirs of being a young girl and reading such books at her mother's side. She also tells of her mother's fear when another Bible smuggling Protestant Mercer, Robert Packington, was shot dead in the street close by to her home.[4]

1 B.L Add. M.S.43827A & B and Add. M.S. 45027 fol.8.
2 Some family trees state December 26th but her portrait at Gainsborough is inscribed with the 27th of December.
3 The Worshipful Company of Mercers is one of the Livery Companies of the City of London.
4 This happened on Monday, Nov. 13th 1536. No one was ever brought to justice for this murder.

Cheapside in the City of London during the Tudor Era.

Rose grew up amongst the daily hustle and bustle of Cheapside at the heart of the London Mercery. The Mercers had their own chapel in Cheapside, sometimes referred to as St. Thomas of Acres[5].

Rose's father owned many properties in the area including a large retail outlet in Cheapside which he called 'The Lock' as well as a grand house in Bow Lane. Many of the frequent great parades and processions of the City of London would pass down this broad thoroughfare of Cheapside, including that of the coronation of Queen Anne Boleyn.

When King Henry VIII sought a divorce from his first wife, Queen Katherine of Aragon, in what later was to become known as the King's *Great Matter*, it was William Locke who imported into England Protestant tracts and translations from the Continent, especially for Anne Boleyn, to put forward in this cause.

However, after the Pope refused to grant King Henry his divorce, the King went ahead with one regardless. In 1534, Henry had Parliament pass two Acts, one to declare that the Pope had no authority in England and secondly to declare that Henry was to be, hence forth, the head of the Church of England.

In angry reaction, Pope Clement VII issued a Papal Bull, which was posted up at Dunkirk in France, proclaiming a curse upon both the King and his country. It was William Locke who succeeded in a most daring and dangerous mission to pull it down. In recognition of this deed, Henry appointed William as his Royal Mercer, made him a 'gentleman of his privy chamber' and also granted William a freehold of £100 per year. The King was also 'vouchsafed' to dine in William Locke's London home – so it is quite possible that Rose also got to meet him.

When plague ravaged the City of London in the summer of 1536, William decided to remove his young family to the safety of Merton, some seven miles outside of the City, south of the river Thames in Surrey.

5 Also known as St. Thomas of Acon.

King Henry VIII- Gainsborough Old Hall.

In 1499, it is known that a John *Lok*[6] and his wife Jane obtained the lease of an estate opposite the parish church of St. Mary the Virgin which in later times was known as Church House.

On October 13th of 1537, eleven-year-old Rose's mother, Katherine, died in childbirth at Merton. Her baby son, named John, died the following day. At about the same time as this tragedy, King Henry's third wife, Jane Seymour, had also been in labour at Hampton Court Palace.

In 1543, seventeen- year old Rose married another of King Henry VIII's favourites, Anthony Hickman. This Hickman family originated in Oxford, but had moved to Woodford in Essex during the early 14th century. Anthony was a London Mercer and merchant adventurer in partnership with Rose's brother, Thomas

During the reign of Edward VI, William Locke was knighted in recognition of his loyalty and service to the late king. William rose to the positions of Sheriff of London and Alderman and continued in a life of high favour until his death in 1550. Sir William was buried in the Mercer's Chapel at Cheapside close to his first wife, parents and other family members.

Rose's Locke Siblings

After the death of Rose's mother, William Locke had remarried twice more, but had no further offspring. Although Sir William had around twenty children in all, sadly more than half of them died in childhood. However, some of Rose's remaining siblings grew up to be quite remarkable adults and all were steadfast, and mostly evangelical, Protestants also.

6 Until fairly recent times, the spelling of the Locke surname has been very fluid at times being spelt by family members as either Lok, Locke or sometimes Lock. Even Rose's siblings are known to have favoured different spellings of their surname for their own personal use.

John Lok (1527-1558)

Rose's older brother, John Lok, was the only one of Sir William's adult sons known not to have become a Mercer. Instead John became an insatiable traveller and adventurer.

We learn from Hakluyt that in 1553, John travelled to Jerusalem - a dangerous and arduous journey in those days.

In 1554 he led a ground breaking expedition to the Portuguese dominated territory of the Gold Coast of Guinea to open up that area to English trade. He returned in 1555 with a cargo that included 400lbs of gold. John Lok is also the first Englishman recorded to have taken slaves (five) from Africa to bring into England.

The date of John's death is thought to have been in 1558 in France.[7]

Thomas Locke (1514-1556)

Like his father, William, Rose's older brother, Thomas Locke, was a successful Mercer and played an active part in the family business. Also like his father, Thomas was much favoured by both King Henry VIII and his son, King Edward VI.

In a letter dated 23rd. June, 1544,[8] (the year that the English invaded France) Thomas writes to King Henry from Antwerp reporting that he has bought and shipped on his Majesty's behalf 76 'bregandynes', and at Brussels he had ordered bespoke 100 pairs of 'pollderons', 'cheyns' for 500 horses, and had loaded on board another ship ready to leave, 40 pairs of 'grevis', 65 pairs of 'maylee slevis' with mail to cover 62 pairs of arming shoes and with enough on order for 100 more. He has also purchased 'corsys of silke' (108 yards) at 2s & 2s.6d per yard.

Thomas and his business partner, Anthony Hickman, jointly financed and especially commissioned a ship to be built which they named the *'Mary Rose'* in honour of their wives. The *'Mary Rose'* later played an important part during the English fight against the Spanish

7 According to *'The Book of Lockes'.*

8 : 'Henry VIII: June 1544, 21-25', Letters and Papers, Foreign and Domestic.

Amada and in a daring raid on Cadiz in 1596. (A second ship, a carrack[9] built in 1559 and also co-owned by Anthony Hickman, called *'The Great Christopher'* was soon purchased by Queen Elizabeth. In September 1562 the Navy renamed this ship *'Victory'* in honour of Protestant success in Scotland. After reconstruction as a galleon in 1585, the *Victory* went on to become the flagship of Sir John Hawkins at the defeat of the Spanish Amada in 1588. This was the first in a succession of Royal Navy ships to bear that name).

After the death of Henry VIII, King Edward VI's government embraced Protestantism and brought about many of the reforms people, like the Locke family, had long campaigned for. Early in 1553, Thomas Locke was able to purchase the advowson of St. Mary the Virgin Church in Merton thus becoming both its benefactor and Rector.

However, King Edward died soon after and Catholic Queen Mary Tudor came to the throne commanding the return of England to the Roman Catholic Church.

Thomas at first refused to submit himself to the Catholic faith. Instead he and Anthony Hickman became involved in helping persecuted Protestants escape from England. They were both arrested.

After a period of imprisonment in the notorious Fleet Prison, Thomas was released a broken man. His wife, Mary, refused to flee the country and so instead of escaping abroad, Thomas remained in England. Outwardly he then appeared to conform to Catholicism, but soon died, much troubled, in October 1556. Mary then became lay rector and patroness of Merton.

Henry Locke (1536-1570)

Rose's younger brother, Henry, was also a Mercer. His wife, Anne, gained notoriety at the time for her very close association with the Scot Presbyterian preacher, John Knox. Knox was also a close friend of Rose Hickman and her husband, Anthony.

John Knox fled England during the reign of Bloody Queen Mary. When he reached Protestant Geneva he wrote back to England pleading to Anne Locke to join him. Eventually,

9 *Carrack or nau* – a three or four masted sailing ship developed by the Portuguese- the first proper ocean-going ships in Europe and the type used to explore the world in the 15th & 16th centuries.

Anne did just that, taking her two young children with her but leaving her husband Henry behind. The couple's young daughter died just two days after reaching Geneva.

In Geneva, Anne Locke translated religious tracts and such like to be smuggled back to Knox's Protestant followers in England. She also wrote many original works herself.

On Anne's return to England, some time shortly after Queen Elizabeth came to the throne, she and her husband Henry appear to have continued their marriage until Henry's death. After this Anne married twice more. Firstly to the evangelical Protestant minister Richard Dering and then in on December 7th, 1579 to Richard *Prowze* at Saint Thomas The Apostle in London.

According to the *'Dictionary of National Biography' Vol 1-20*, Henry and Anne's 'third son' was Henry Locke 'the poet', born around 1554-58 . A number of sonnets, poems and other works attributed to him are listed in full in the above directory (page 91-92).

Between the ages of sixteen and twenty-one, Henry Locke junior is thought to have spent some time at Oxford, although he does not seem to have matriculated at the university, and there is no record of him having taken a degree. After leaving Oxford, Locke sought patronage at court. In 1591 he contributed a sonnet to King James VI of Scotland's 'Essayes of a Prentice'.

After this time, Henry is found persistently petitioning for some position or another at court. In 1597 he was encouraged by the Countess of Warwick to apply to Sir Robert Cecil for 'some pension till an office of forfeiture fell to his relief'. He eventually obtained some confidential employment with Cecil and spent the spring of 1599 at Bayonne collecting intelligence. However, he raised the suspicions of the local inhabitants and as a result found his life in danger.

The following year Henry is found living in the Strand, London after having apparently fallen out of favour with Cecil whom he implored to 'employ him again in secret service at foreign ports'.

In 1606, Henry Locke was imprisoned as an insolvent debtor in the Westminster Gatehouse, and again in May 1608 at the Clink in Southwark under similar circumstances.

Henry is known to have married Ann Moyle of Cornwall and the couple had two sons, Henry born in 1592 and Charles.

Michael Lok (1532 – about 1616)

Michael Lok was to become a widely travelled man like his older brother, John. In *The Book of Lockes* the author states, at the time of his writing, that *'in the Cottonian Library is a manuscript of 'many pages' dated 1577 written by Michael Lok. In this manuscript Michael states that he is son of Wm. Lok, Knight, Alderman of London' that he (Michael) was kept in schools of grammar in England until he was 13, when he was sent overseas to Flanders and France to learn their languages, and to know the world, since which time he has continued these 32 years to travel in body and mind, following his vocation in the trade of merchandize, passing through many countries, had the charge of and captain of a great ship of more than 1000 tons, three years in diverse voyages; and that he has more than 200 sheets of manuscript of his travels, which he wishes to publish.'*

This account gives an intriguing insight into how young boys were brought up and educated to become Mercers at that time. It is very likely that Rose's oldest son, William, received the same sort of grounding, as is evident from part of her reminiscences.

From his youth, Michael Lok became obsessed with finding a North-West passage through to China via the New World. It was a venture that would eventually bring him into partnership with an unscrupulous Martin Frobisher and lead him to utter ruination, bankruptcy and numerous spells as a debtor inside the prisons of London.

In January 1579, Michael can be found petitioning the Privy Council for relief and assistance [10].He writes that for the past three years he has taken charge of all the business of Martin Frobisher's voyages; of his own money he has expended some 7,500l ' all the goods he had in the world, whereby himself, his wife, and fifteen children are left to beg for their bread.'

As a result of this petition, in February 1579 he was allowed 403l. However, by June 1581, he can be found again imprisoned, at the Fleet, and once more petitioning the council . This time it was as the result of the suit of William Burgh to pay 200l. for a ship purchased for Frobisher's last voyage, *'which is not the prisoner's debt'.* Michael was also bound for a debt of

10 Calendar of State Papers, East Indies.

almost a further 3,000l, *'still owing by the company of adventurers'.*

It is not known when Michael was eventually released from prison, but he appears not to have recovered his money.

Michael was in Dublin, Ireland in 1587-8, and in 1592 as consul for the Levant Company to Aleppo for four years. Two years into this appointment Michael's services were suddenly dispensed with, in his own words *'by the intrigues of one Dorrington, in the employment of Sir John Spencer, alderman of London.'*[11] Michael subsequently claimed the salary for the full four years and in 1599 can be found still claiming it- although it appears he was never paid.

In 1603, Michael's son, Zachary Lok, died. In his will he bequeathed his seal of arms to his father. In May 1605, Michael's son Eleazer *'Loke'* died , leaving *'to my father twenty-six pounds a year, payable quarterly...my father shall have my gown and best black cloak and my seal ring'.*

In June, 1608, Michael can be found sending intelligence *'of the war-like preparations being made by the King of Spain'* to the Earl of Salisbury.

Michael was married twice- first to Joan, daughter of William Wilkinson, Sheriff of London. Joan died in 1571. Eight of her and Michael's children from that marriage are named in her will.[12] Michael's second wife was Mary or Margaret, daughter of Martin *Perient*,[13] treasurer to the army in Ireland. Mary was the widow of Caesar Adelmare and mother of a prominent judge- Sir Julius Caesar.

'An conveniens sit Matrimonium inter Puellam et Senem'[14], written by Michael in 1583 might suggest that he was contemplating marrying for a third time in his old age. Amongst his other writings, Lok translated part of Peter Martyr's *'Historie of the West Indies'* into English which was published in 1612.

Michael's son, Benjamin *'Locke'* of London, died and his will proved on 29th August 1611. In it he states that *'I give and bequeath to my father Michael Locke thirty pounds and do further release and discharge him of and for all such debts and sums of money as he oweth me*

11 Add. M.S 12497; Zachary Lok to Cecil,9 December 1598,in Calendar of .State Papers, Domestic..)

12 Will dated 9th Feb 1571, proved by Lok April 6th 1571.

13 Alternatively - Margery Peryn, Widow of Caesar Dalmarias, MD of Venice (father of Sir Julius Caesar, Knight).

14 Add. M.S. 12058.

by speciality bill bond or otherwise'

As late as 1614-15, Michael was still being pursued for a debt of 200l due for stores supplied for Frobisher's ships. Michael Lok was by then eighty-three years old and is thought to have died shortly thereafter.

Matthew Locke (1521-1552)

Very little is known about the life of Matthew Locke. He lived to adulthood and his will was proved on May 27th 1552. His wife, Elizabeth Baker died a year before him.

Rose and Anthony Hickman's life together

Rose's brother, Thomas, and her husband, Anthony, were very successful in their joint trading enterprise. They kept agents or 'factors' on the Continent and especially in the Canary Islands where they traded in sugar and expensive spices.

During the reign of Edward VI, Thomas Locke and Rose and Anthony Hickman gave financial support and encouragement to such well known Protestants as Bishop Hooper, John Foxe and John Knox, amongst others and continued to do so after the death of Edward and the accession of his Catholic half-sister, Queen Mary.

As a result of helping many leading Protestants and their families to escape from persecution, both Anthony and Thomas were imprisoned in the infamous Fleet prison in London. According to Rose's own account, the pair were already in the Fleet when the entire jury in the case of treason against Sir Nicholas Throckmorton were also consigned there on April 17th 1554, for daring to find the defendant innocent.

Though Thomas and Anthony were eventually released, it was thought prudent for the pair to flee to the Low Countries. Anthony Hickman already enjoyed the use of several houses there. Unfortunately Thomas's wife, Mary was against this, and so Rose's brother was forced to remain in England with her.

Rose had no such qualms about getting her own family to Antwerp and safety. However, Rose was by this time pregnant with her fifth child. Not wanting to jeopardise the life of her unborn baby by risking a rough sea crossing, she managed to persuade Anthony to flee the country without her - the intention being that she would join with him as soon as the expected child was safely delivered.

After Anthony's departure, Rose writes that she went to 'Chilswell'[15] near Oxford to await the birth of her child. Whilst doing so, she corresponded with the now imprisoned Anglican clergymen, Cranmer, Latimer, and Ridley about the validity of Catholic baptism.

They advised her that, in their opinion, the Catholic baptism was the *least corrupted* of the Papist ceremonies, but also that it might be best for Rose to flee abroad *before* the need for the child to be baptised.

Whether Rose presented the baby *voluntarily* for baptism after the birth or not remains unclear. However Rose writes in her memoir of how she substituted a handkerchief full of sugar in place of the salt that she was expected to supply the priest with for the ceremony. Thus the ritual was rendered invalid.

After this, Rose escape from England to join Anthony in Antwerp. There were several advantages in the choice of this city. Anthony could carry on with his business activities and thus continue to support not only his own family but also to help other Protestants fleeing England. He could also maintain his contact with other Mercers and friends back in England.

More importantly, unlike the English system of worship in small parish churches, in Antwerp everyone attended mass in a vast Cathedral instead, making it much easier to absent oneself from services unnoticed. However, being discovered to be a Protestant by the authorities in Catholic ruled Antwerp was just as dangerous as it was to be in England.

From her own account, we know that another of Rose and Anthony's children was born during this exile. Rose tells how a strip of cloth was hung outside at her door after the birth of this child. Research has found that this custom in Antwerp[16] of hanging out a piece of cloth after the birth of a child was only done in the case of a male baby.

15 Probably *Chilswell Farm,* Cumnor near Oxford

16 The Travel Journal of Antonio de Beatis-Edited by Hale and Lindon (The Hakluyt Society 1979)

Again Rose wanted to avoid a Catholic baptism for her newborn. She managed to find an underground network of local Protestants to take her baby to have it baptised in secret according to their own reformist doctrine. However, this was extremely dangerous as the local magistrate had earned a dreadful reputation for hunting out babies suspected of not having been baptized into the Catholic faith, placing them in sacks and throwing them into the River Scheldt to drown. It was a fate that could have equally befallen Rose's baby had it been discovered.

Rose's family remained in Antwerp until the death of Queen Mary and the ascension of Protestant Queen Elizabeth I to the English throne. Shortly after her return to London, Rose gave birth to another son. Altogether, she and Anthony had six known sons and a daughter.

Mary Hickman

Rose's eldest child, *'Marye'* Hickman, was baptized at St. Olave Old Jewry in London on the 6th of January 1547, just a few weeks before the death of King Henry VIII. This church was not far from the Mercer's Chapel in Ironmonger Lane and the family's London home in Cheapside.

Mary Hickman reached adulthood and in most known genealogical family trees is listed as being thought to have married a man named Ansham of Ealing[17], before subsequently marrying a *Richard Philips* of Middlesex.

During my own research, I have found a marriage entry for Marye Hickman dated 13th April 1567 at Saint Olave Old Jewry in London to one John Amondesham. Amondesham is an earlier form of the name Aunsham, and unsurprisingly there was an established Mercer family of the same name at the time. Mary's second marriage was to Richard Phillips. At the time there was also an established Philips family amongst the Mercery.

By this second husband, Mary is described[18] as having had 'divers sons and daughters & dyed long before her mother- leaving these sons and daughters following viz., Jerome Philips

17 BL Add MS 45027 records this husband as *'Agmonsham [sic] Ansham Esq'.*
18 BL Add MS 45027

B.D yet living[19], William Phillips-a Lieutenant in ye wars in ye Low Countries in the time of King James who there took to wife a Norfolk Gentlewoman called Rose Rookwood, sister of Captain Rookwood'. Also 'this William Phillips dyed in Breda when it was besieged by Marquis Spinola[20], leaving two daughters by this said wife'. A son, Edward Phillips, Gent. - who is yet living' and 'Richard Phillips, a merchant, who using traffique into France is there married & dwelleth at a town called Abierill'. A daughter, Anne Phillips, 'who was married to Walter Cary, Clerk, which said Anne dyed in the year 1628 leaving six sons & a daughter all living at this time.'

The manuscript goes on to add that Lady Rose 'saw with her eyes before her departure four of these sons,' and that her epitaph truly claims 'she did her children's children's children see.'

Finally is Rose Phillips, who was married to William Toll (deceased by 1637) by whom she had three sons and a daughter- the sons were all dead by 1637 but the daughter was still alive and living with her mother.

19 In 1637, the time that this copy of Rose's memoirs is thought to have been written.

20 Between August 1624 & June 1625.

William Hickman

Rose's second child and eldest son was William. He was born in London and baptized on June 16th 1549 at St. Olave Old Jewry in London. From a young age, William seems to have developed a knack for escaping impending death. We learn from Rose's account that when William was five or six he became very ill one night and almost died. Luckily his father, Anthony, was able to get some medicine into the boy whose teeth had 'locked tightly together'. However, in the process several of the child's milk teeth were lost.

When he was a schoolboy, William climbed up onto the roof of a house and fell off! Miraculously he escaped unharmed. He also narrowly escaped drowning in a river during his childhood.

As the oldest son, it was natural that William should grow up to follow in his father's footsteps as a Mercer and so he would have been sent abroad to learn his trade and other languages.

When he was about nineteen years of age, Rose writes that William accompanied Queen Elizabeth's Ambassador, Mister Randal, on a trading mission to the Emperor of Russia - Ivan the Terrible.

When the ships stopped en route to Moscow, to let the gentlemen stretch their legs, William was accidentally left ashore somewhere along the bleak Russian coastline. Luckily his absence was noticed and a search party sent ashore found him before night fell. Had they not, then he would have been in grave danger of being eaten by hungry bears or wolves.

On March 17th, 1593, William married Agnes or 'Anne' Dixie at St Michael, Bassishaw in London. (The medieval pronunciation of Agnes was 'Annis' and its usage and many of its forms coincided with the equally popular English name Anne, a name commonly thought to be related to Agnes or even versions of the same name).

Agnes was the daughter of Christopher Draper, Lord Mayor of London and widow of Sir Wolstan Dixie. An 'Anne' Draper is recorded as having married a *'Wolstan Dixby'* on June 20th,

1569 at St Dunstan-In-The-East, London. Agnes had no issue by either Sir Wolstan or William.

In February 1600, Agnes died and William remarried very quickly. His second wife was Elizabeth Willoughby, the daughter of Lord Willoughby of Parham - a strong Puritan family. Over the next ten years, William and Elizabeth had six children; Anne 1601-1602, Frances, 1602-, Willoughby 1604-1649, William 1606- 1607, Thomas 1607-, Mildred 1610-1628.

William died in 1625, a few months after the death of King James I.

Portrait of William Hickman- Gainsborough Old Hall.
Photograph by Roger Vorhauer.

Henry Hickman

Rose's second son, Henry was baptised on December 7th, 1550 at St. Olave Old Jewry, in London. Henry was a gifted student and after attending St. Paul's School in the city, went on to St. John's College Cambridge.

In 1573, Henry and some other fellows compiled a list of complaints against their master and successfully had him removed. Henry became Proctor in 1584.

Henry appears also to have enjoyed acting as his name appears on a cast list of a comedy performed there called *Hymenaeus* in 1579. Some scholars think that he may even have written it. The following year, in a production of Dr. Legge's Latin play about Richard III, Henry played the part of Henry, Earl of Richmond.

After a distinguished career at Cambridge, Henry became a Doctor of Law and a civil lawyer. He was Chancellor for the Diocese of Peterborough (1587); J.P.Q Northamptonshire by 1592; Freeman of Northampton and Master in Chancery 1602-16.

At his own request of the corporation of Northampton, in 1601 Henry was returned for the forthcoming election and became its Member of Parliament. The assembly at the time noted that he was 'well acquainted with the state of this town, and assert[s] the good thereof ... for all a long time having been an inhabitant'.

Also in 1601, Henry married Anne Wallop, daughter of Richard Wallop of Bugbrooke, Northamptonshire and widow of one Mister Eccleston, of Eccleston, Lancashire. They had a son named Anthony who died in 1647 and two daughters, Elizabeth and Anne.

According to the third copy of Rose's manuscript, Elizabeth married *'Sir Henry Feines, Knight, one of the sons of the Earl of Lincoln'* and Anne married Richard Dukeson, Rector of St. Clements.

In his 'Memoirs of the Life of Sir Henry Fynes, alias Clinton, Knight', Elizabeth's husband writes none too fondly about his Hickman wife. (His first wife had died after childbirth and Henry Fynes remained unmarried for about a year afterwards).

'But it pleased God, for sins and offences, to put thoughts into my head of marriage.

*- Well I **** after my worldly reasons, and married the daughter of Henry Hickman, Doctor of the Civil Law, finding her at Gainsborough, at her uncle's, Sir William Hickman's, and brought myself by her a world of afflictions; for she proved so jealous, so melancholy, so angry, peevish, and captious, so proud and conceited, and so full of devilish and un-reformable humours.'*

In assessing the validity of these complaints, it is helpful to read the rest of Sir Henry's account about himself and his life.

According to Maddison's Lincolnshire Pedigrees, Henry Hickman made a will dated 4th February 1616 that was proved at Peterborough on the 4th September 1618. In it he stated that he wished to be buried at Gainsborough.

Walter Hickman

'Watter' Hickman was baptised at St. Olave Old Jewry in London on the 26th August 1552.

Walter's early life path remains unknown, but unlike his brothers Henry and Anthony, who made careers in the legal profession, he remained within the London world of business.

Walter married Elizabeth Staines of Essex, the daughter of Nicholas Staines, Mercer, on the 21st November in 1586. They had three sons, William, Walter and Dixie, and one daughter named Elizabeth. William and Walter (a Captain in the Low Countries) [21]died unmarried.

Another London Mercer, Sir Wolstan Dixie, was godfather to Dixie Hickman who was baptized on 8th January, 1589 at St. Stephan Church, Coleman St, London.

According to the third copy of Rose Hickman's manuscript, Sir Wolstan is described as being *'sometime Lord Mayor of London, and had his chiefest education and the best means of his first setting up his trade in his youth from this old Gentlewoman's said husband, Mister Anthony Hickman, whose kinsman he was.'*

The only connection to date that I have been able to find between Anthony Hickman and Wolstan Dixie to explain any family relationship is the fact that Anthony's mother was Alice Jephson of Froyle and Wolstan's mother was an 'Anne' Jephson. The two women may have been sisters, especially as they both appear to have had fathers named William.

Later, in 1616, Dixie Hickman married Elizabeth, the daughter of Sir William, 5th Lord Windsor. Later the Earls of Plymouth descended through this line.

Walter Hickman's daughter, Elizabeth, first married George Alington of Swinhope at Gainsborough and then William Painter Esq. and *'dyed leaving issue by both her husbands'.*

At the age of twenty-five, Walter purchased a wardship – of one John Leigh- who in turn, soon became the stepson of Sir William Killigrew, Groom of the Privy Chamber to Queen Elizabeth and later to King James I. Walter remained involved in Leigh's personal affairs.

In 1586, Walter can be found investing in property in London, and during 1591-2 was

21 BL Add MS 45027.

shipping tin to London from Cornwall.

Walter was a man who certainly had capital at his disposal and is known to have advanced £500 to his brother-in-law to help obtain him an office. However, a similar offer to Sir Robert Cecil in 1594 failed to secure the receivership of the Court of Wards for his brother, William. In 1590, Walter Hickman and his brothers obtained a grant of arms.

By 1593 Walter can be found living in Kew, near to Richmond Palace. It was an area popular with courtiers. Walter later obtained the rights to the ferry crossing at Kew over the River Thames (there was no bridge there at the time) and can be found continuing to consolidate property there in 1610. He is also sometimes described as being 'Walter Hickman of Kew and at others as 'of St. Dustan's-in-the-West,' in London. Walter Hickman is also listed as being a Justice of the Peace in the Middlesex rolls[22].

In 1602, Walter and John Leigh jointly received a royal grant of property in Devon and Cornwall. By the time of Queen Elizabeth's death the following year, Walter had become a Gentleman Usher but did not retain the post under the incoming King James. Nonetheless, he is thought to have maintained a presence at court.

Walter did, however, succeed Sir William Killigrew to become Surveyor of Crown lands, Middlesex and London from 1606 – 16. He was also The Keeper of the Seal Office of the King's Bench and Common Pleas by this time and a Commissioner for aliens in London.

Walter's son, Dixie, became a gentleman Usher to Princess Elizabeth by 1612 and is known to have travelled with her to Heidelberg in April 1613. Another member of that party is recorded as being *'Mr. Hickman'* – and was possibly Walter, as he is known to have taken out one year's life assurance in September 1612, just prior to the arrival of Elizabeth's future husband, the Elector Palatine in England, having come to claim his bride.

In December 1613, Walter was appointed to a Middlesex commission and in 1614 he became Member of Parliament for Mitchell.

According to Maddison, in February 1616, Walter witnessed his brother, Henry's, will (although Henry subsequently lived until September 1618). However, on December 23rd, 1617

22 From September 1617 until his death.

Walter himself fell sick and drew up his own will. He died a week later in expectation of salvation through Christ's merits *'and by no other means whatsoever'.*

A fine, but damaged monument to Walter Hickman can be found in the church of St. Mary Magdalene at Richmond, Surrey where his wife and sons are also buried. The inscription on it states that Walter died in 1617. However, a blank has been left for the number of years that he had lived, probably because those erecting the monument did not know the date of Walter's birth, but hoped that it might become available later.

Portrait of Walter Hickman – Gainsborough Old Hall.
Photograph by Roger Vorhauer.

Anthony Hickman Junior

Anthony Hickman was baptised on 17th November 1560 at St. Olave Old Jewry, London.

According to an entry in Alumni Cantabrigienses (Venn, J & Venn, JA, Cambridge 1924), *'Anthony Hickman matriculated, pensioner*[23] *from St. John's Michaelmas 1575, 4th s. of Anthony, of Woodford Hall, Essex. Migrated to Peterhouse, B.A., 1579-80; M.A. 1583; L.L.D. Fellow of Corpus Christi, 1583 -8, where he had a long dispute with the College. Adm., advocate, June 16, 1583.'*

This 'long dispute' at Cambridge arose after there was an objection raised by a new Master, Doctor Copcot, coming into Corpus Christi. This related to Anthony Hickman having had a special dispensation, signed by Queen Elizabeth, which in effect 'excused' him from taking orders - a normal requirement of one taking up a Fellowship. At one point Anthony found himself ejected from his rooms and for a time also deprived of his Fellowship. (Original transcripts of portions of the correspondence relating to this matter can be found amongst the Portland Papers, currently held at Longleat House, including one written by Archbishop Whitgift and another in Anthony's own hand and bearing his signature).

Puritans at that time had no objection to becoming ordained in the Church of England, even those like John Robinson and Richard Clyfton who later broke away to become Separatists. Therefore the question remains as to why Anthony Hickman objected? It is certainly possible that he should have resisted ordination on the grounds of disapproval of the Elizabethan Church settlement in much the same way as the Presbyterians did- leading one to strongly speculate that perhaps Anthony Hickman was himself a Separatist.

Interestingly, Mayflower Pilgrim William Brewster matriculated December 3rd, 1580 at Peterhouse (before entering the service of William Davidson in 1583). Leading Separatist, Robert 'Troublechurch' Browne, was also resident at Cambridge at the same time as both Brewster and Anthony Hickman.

Although this dispute was eventually settled in Anthony's favour, in 1592 he found himself

23 'Pensioner' means that his father could afford to pay for his food or commons and defray other expenses.

again under attack by the new incoming master, Dr. John Jegon. Anthony left Corpus Christi the following year. (Incidentally, the John Jegon who had been the bane of Anthony's final years at Cambridge later became the bishop of Norwich and in turn deprived John Robinson of his living. Robinson was Pastor to, and a leading figure of the Separatists' Congregation in Leiden.)

Anthony Hickman became a Doctor of the Civil Law. He died, unmarried, in London on December 13th in 1597. He was buried in the Church of St. Bennet, Paul's Wharf which was destroyed in the great fire of London in 1666.

Anthony Hickman - private collection.
Photograph by Roger Vorhauer.

Eleazar Hickman

'Elyesar' Hickman was baptised on the 3rd of April, 1562 at St. Olave Old Jewry in London. Relatively little is known about the lives of either of Rose's two youngest sons, although both are known to have lived until adulthood.

According to British Library Additional Manuscript 45027, (the aforementioned third but much later version of Rose Hickman's memoirs, thought to have been written around 1637 and including some family genealogy), Eleazar was 'Gentleman Usher to Ludovic Stuart, Duke of Lennox and of Richmond' (1574-1624), and 'died without issue.' Maddison notes that Eleazar 'of St. Martin's–in- the-Field, Middlesex was a witness to his brother Walter's will made on December 28th 1618. Eleazar's date of death is uncertain.

Matthew Hickman

At the time of writing no record of Matthew Hickman's baptism has yet been found. According to the third, later copy of Rose Hickman's memoires, a brief genealogy has been added listing the three children of Matthew as; Frances, Mary and Rose, and that Frances was already deceased by 1637 but that the remaining two at that date were still living. The identity of their mother is not known. Matthew is also described as being a 'clerk' and it is stated that he had *'dyed since his mother.'*

Unknown Children born at Chilswell and Antwerp.

In her memoir, Rose writes about two of her children's birth in particular and yet does not record their names. The identity of the child born to Rose at Chilswell, near Oxford around 1554/5 remains unknown at the time of writing.

Rose and Anthony's third son was Walter, born in 1552. Rose's fourth son is known from contemporary records to be Anthony, born in 1560. Therefore the child that was born to Rose while in Antwerp cannot be either of these. His birth must have fallen somewhere between 1556 and 1559 and as he was baptized secretly and *illegally* as a Protestant in Catholic ruled Antwerp, it is understandable that no record of his birth can be found.

The Throckmorton Marriage

When Rose's first husband, Anthony Hickman, died in 1573, Rose remarried. Her second husband was a widower, Simon Throckmorton of Brampton.

Interestingly, in Rose's portrait of 1596 she is categorically inscribed as being 'Rose Hickman', when in fact she was still officially 'Rose Throckmorton'.

In Rose Hickman's memoires of 1610, she describes herself as *'Rose Throckmorton - widow late of Simon Throckmorton'.* Yet in a duplicate copy of those writings (written in a different hand and inscribed at the bottom of the page with the words Elizabeth Hickman) after the mention of the name Anthony Hickman is the addition of the words *'by whom I had all my children'* as if to perhaps 'distance' the Hickmans from the tainted Throckmorton name.

Simon Throckmorton was born around 1526. His father, Richard Throckmorton of Higham Ferrars, Northants, had been a brother to Sir George Throckmorton (d 1553) of Coughton Court, Warwickshire. Sir George had been a knight in Henry VIII's household but vehemently opposed to the King's break with Rome.

Although the vast majority of Sir George's nineteen children, and over one hundred grandchildren, were ardent Catholics there were some, however, who were strongly Protestant. (Among these had been his grandson, Sir Nicholas Throckmorton, who had been in the Fleet Prison with Rose's husband and brother).

Robert Throckmorton, Sir George's heir, married his children into the leading Catholic families of the time and many members of this extended Catholic Throckmorton family became involved in plots against the Protestant throne of England.

Two of Sir Robert's daughters, Anne and Muriel, were the mothers of men involved in the Gunpowder Plot of 1605 against King James- Robert Catesby and Francis Tresham. A third daughter, Mary, was the wife of Edward Arden, executed in 1583 for his part in a failed assassination attempt against Queen Elizabeth. Another family member, Francis Throckmorton, was executed in 1584 for acting as a go-between for Mary Queen of Scots and the Spanish Ambassador in yet another plot.

Simon Throckmorton purchased the manor of Gerard Foster, in Brampton, on the outskirts of Huntingdon in 1550. He was twice elected to Parliament during the reign of Queen Mary but 'disappears' from the Commons in 1559 after which he passed the remainder of his life in comparative obscurity.

It is, however, strongly suspected that Simon Throckmorton was a Catholic which would explain why he failed to secure a position as even a Justice of the Peace under Queen Elizabeth. He had also been strongly associated with Sir Robert Tyrwhitt, whom Elizabeth had been interrogated by during her suspected liaison with Thomas Seymour.

Rose and Simon Throckmorton lived at Brampton until Simon's death on March 27th, 1585 when the estate passed to his eldest son, Robert. Rose had no children by this second marriage.

Frances Throckmorton, the daughter of Simon Throckmorton, married Wolstan Dixie of Brampton (a nephew of Sir Wolstan Dixie) at St James' Church, Clerkenwell, London on January 28th, 1598.

Rose in Later Life

In 1593 *the Act Against Puritans* was passed making life for religious dissenters in England more difficult than ever. In that same year, two prominent Separatists, John Greenwood and Henry Barrow were executed in London. John Greenwood had been at Corpus Christi at the same time as Rose's son, Anthony.

After the death of Rose's second husband, Simon, she moved to Gainsborough Hall in Lincolnshire sometime in 1596 with her son, William and his wife, Agnes.
It is unclear whether the fear of a renewed religious persecution, or William's failure to secure the receivership of the Court of Wards prompted Puritan Rose and William Hickman's decision to leave the confines of London.

Whatever the reason, Gainsborough Hall became the family's main residence and William conducted much of his business from the town's busy port. He increased the thrice yearly fairs to encourage 'outside' traders and goods into the town. This may have angered local merchants greatly to see their own prices undercut, but this move could have broken any existing local monopoly and allowed the natural forces of supply and demand to come into play, and may have served to drive down the cost of living for the poor of the town. However, there is evidence that many of the local Gainsborough nobles and gentry, many of whom were either conservative Anglicans or covert Catholics, despised William as an 'incomer' and resented his Puritan stance and his moves to reform trading practices in the town.

As stated previously, Agnes Hickman died in February 1600 and William swiftly remarried. He and his new wife soon had the first of six children together. When a local Separatist, a former Anglican preacher named John Smyth, needed a place for his congregation to meet in secret, Rose and William are believed to have accommodated them at the Hall.

In 1603 when King James I ascended the throne of England, William Hickman rode out to greet the new monarch as he travelled south on the Great North Road to London. In return for this early sign of allegiance, William was knighted at Belvoir Castle.

John Smyth's Separatist congregation fled from England sometime around 1606/07. Shortly after they had fled to Holland, the first of two escape attempts were made by William Brewster's Scrooby congregation at Boston in the autumn of 1607. This failed and resulted in some of the men being arrested for a time.

Brewster and the congregation made a second attempt to flee England from the Humber in the spring of 1608 which proved successful. It is quite possible that these Separatists may have been helped on both occasions by the Hickmans.

Rose Hickman lived until 1613 and was buried in the local parish church.

Gainsborough Old Hall. Photograph by Roger Vorhauer.

Monuments and Memorials

There are very few surviving monuments to members of the Locke and Hickman families of this era. Rose's husband, Anthony, and many other members of the Locke family, are known to have been interred in the Mercers Chapel in London. Sadly all traces of their burials were destroyed during the Great Fire of London in 1666. Likewise many London church records were also lost at that time.

Many of these relatives left wills, some of which have survived, stating their express wishes to be buried within the Mercers' Chapel in the City of London, which we have no reason to believe were not carried out. At that time, will-making was very much a part of the dying process, and so the probability is that once a person was ill enough to contemplate drawing up a will and decided upon a place, usually within a reasonable distance, to be buried one's wishes were normally carried out.

Sir William Locke, contrary to some Locke genealogy websites, was buried in the Mercers Chapel and a contemporary account of his funeral survives. Many female members of Mercer families were also buried in this chapel, including Sir William's first wife, Alice Spence, and also Mary (Long) Locke – Rose's sister in law.

The crumbling Gainsborough parish church of Lord Burgh's time is now gone, apart from its medieval tower. When the main body of the church was replaced by the beautiful, present Georgian building, any older memorials that might have been placed in the original floor were lost. However, the crypt below remained accessible up until the 1950's when it was bricked up to dissuade the attempts of vandals who had tried to get into it. Last eye witness reports, some from within the clergy of that time, claim to have seen the burials of both Burghs and Hickmans still evident below and possibly some also of the Knights Templar, who it is believed had an earlier church upon the same site before the medieval structure was built.

The following epitaph was written for Rose by members of her own family in 1637.

'God gave unto this matron in her dayes,

As pledges firm of his afflictions [sic] deare

Such happy blessings as the psalmist sayes

They shall receive as serves the Lord in feare.

Her self in wedlock as fruitful as the vine

Her children like the olive plants to be.

And of her issue in descendant line

She did her children's', children's' children see.

And freed of the Babilonish awe

Peace permanent on Israel saw.

Now having fought a good and Christian fight

Against the spiritual common enemy

And excercis'd her self both day and night,

In oracles divine continually.

And kept the sacred faith with constancy

Even in the midst of persecutions rage

Express'd by worthy works of piety

From time to time as well in youth as age.

She finished her course and doth possess

In heavenly bliss the crown of righteousness.'

Rose tells us that her family were staying at Merton in 1537 in order to avoid the plague still raging in the City. In 1499, it is known that a *John Lok* and his wife Jayne obtained the lease of an estate opposite the church which in later times was known as Church House. Lockes would continue to reside there in Merton for at least one hundred and forty years after.

Today no memorials survive inside St. Mary's Church in Merton dedicated to the Lockes.

Much of the interior of the church was laid to tiles, probably in the Victorian era, and so any slabs that may have existed are probably *lost* beneath those.

However, I am eternally grateful to fellow Locke enthusiast, Lionel Green, for the following information. According to John Aubrey, who recorded all of the memorials in St. Mary's Church in 1673,[24] Sir William Locke arranged for a brass plaque to be inset within a marble gravestone which bore the following words:

Pray for the Soule of Kateryn Lok,
sumtyme the Wife of William Lok,
Mercer of London, who decessed the
xiii of October, Anno xv xxxvij. On
Whose Soule Jhesu have Mercy. Amen.

24 J. Aubrey '*The Natural History and Antiquities of the County of Surrey 1718/19 Vol.1 p.224*'.

Interior St. Mary the Virgin, Merton.
Photograph David Reeves.

Parish records from before 1559, the end of the Marian era, no longer survive at Merton. However, below are a few of the earliest Locke burials recorded after that date. These may be of interest to family historians.

1608 October 18th.... A man son of Thomas Lock Esquire.

1613 Sept 23 Lock, Edmund sonne of Thomas Lock Esquire.

1619 April Lock, Mrs Elizabeth gentm.

1621 November 30th Locke ffrancis, gent.

1633 December 26th Lock Thomas, sonne of Thomas Lock Esquire.

1647 February 6th Locke, Mr. Thomas Esquire.

On the north wall of the parish church of St. Mary Magdalene, Richmond, Surrey is a very colourful memorial to Walter Hickman erected sometime after his death in 1617 by his son, Dixie. Walter was one of the original Vestrymen of Richmond in 1614, and took an active part in local affairs. Dixie Hickman, married the eldest daughter of Henry, Lord Windsor, and through her was descended the Earls of Plymouth. The inscription reads;

Memoriæ Sacrum

Here under resteth ye bodie of Walter Hickman of Kewe in this Pish. Esq. who had, By his wife Elizabeth, the daughter of Nicholas Stanes of ye County of Essex 3 Sonnes viz. Dixie, Married unto Elizabeth Windsor Eldest Daughter unto the Right Hon. Henry Lord Windsor; William & Walter Unmarried; & one Daughter named Elizabeth married unto George Alington ye younger of Swinhop in ye county of Lincoln Esq. He lived ---- yeares and on the xxix day of December 1617 he exchanged this mortal life for a better expectinge a joyfull Ressurection.

Dixius Hickman, Armiger ejus primogenitus Et filius mæstissmus, hoc Monumentum posuit.

Memorial to Walter Hickman at Richmond, Surrey.

Part of the inscription, clearly intended to give Walter's age at his death in 1617, is left empty.

Walter's son, William Hickman died in childhood and was buried on 24th January, 1593 at St. Mary Magdalene. Dixie was buried there on 10th October 1631 and an 'Elizabeth Hickman' was buried shortly after on November 2nd - this is most likely to be Dixie's wife.

Inside the redundant Holy Trinity Old Church, Wentworth, South Yorkshire, above the door is a large monument effusively praising Sir William Rokeby of Skiers, and his wife, Frances Hickman. Frances was the granddaughter of Lady Rose Hickman, and featured heavily in my first novel, *The Mayflower Maid.* According to the monument, she was married to William Rokeby for fifty years, and so obviously inherited Rose's longevity (a marriage entry for Frances *'of Bawtry'* and William *'of Hotham'* appears in the Yorkshire registry for 1624).

There are many other Rokeby monuments to be found at Kirk Sandall, near Doncaster, another redundant church which, like Wentworth, is in the care of the Churches Conservation Trust.

Rokeby memorial at Wentworth – photograph by Roger Vorhauer.

Here follows simplified extracts from both the Hickman and Locke family trees.

Offspring of **Walter Hickman**, of Woodford Hall

Walter b. about 1480 - d 1540
m. Alice Jephson or Jepherson of Froyle

1. William
2. Dorothea
3. Anthony (3rd son)
   m. Rose Locke
4. Clement

Walter directed in his will that he be buried at Woodford. He bequeathed to Clement, his fourth son, four of his best ambling mares, his best gown lined with stitches, and his best russet gown lined with fox.

To the church at Woodford, he left £10 for the purpose of redeeming paschal money at Easter, so that every body in the parish, being free from the payment of the same, when they came to God's board, might say a *Pater noster* and *Ave* for his soul, and all Christian souls. - *'The Environs of London: Vol.4'* by Daniel Lysons 1796.

Family Tree of Sir William Locke showing Rose Hickman's Line

Sir William Lok was the son of Thomas Lok, Mercer of London, and grandson of John Lok, Sheriff of London in 1460 (c.f. will of Zachary Lok, 1603) [25]. From the grandfather also descended John Locke, Mayor of Bristol in 1642, who was 'a sort of cousin' of the father of John Locke [q.v.] the philosopher.

Sir William Locke, Knight and Alderman of London, b.1480- d.1550 and buried at Mercers' Chapel, London.

m1. **Alice Spence** of London b about 1490 - d.1522 (buried at Mercer's Chapel, London)

1. **William Locke** b.1511 - d.1517
2. **Philip Locke** d.1524
3. **Jayne Locke** b. Aug 29th, 1512
   m. Robert Meredith of London, mercer
4. **Peter Locke** d.1517
5. **William Locke** b.1517 - d.1519
6. **Richard Locke** d.1516
7. **Edmund Locke** b.? d.1545 for the love of Sir Brian Tuck's daughter.
8. **Thomas Locke** b. Feb 8th, 1514 – d 30th October, 1556 merchant, (Buried Mercers Chapel)
   m. Mary Lounge or Long b.1518 - d 1578. (Buried Mercers Chapel).
   Married at St. Peter's Church, Cheapside, London 19th January 1544
9. **Matthew Locke** b.1521- d.1552 merchant
   m. Elizabeth Baker (d.1551)

m2. **Katherine Cook** (dau. of Sir Thomas Cook of Wiltshire, Knight) d. Oct 14th, 1537, buried at Merton

1. **Dorothy Locke** b. –
   m1. Otwell Hill of London, mercer
   m2. John Cosworth of London, merchant.
2. **Katherine Locke** b.-
   m1. Thomas Stacey of London, mercer.
   m2. William Matthew of Braden, Northamptonshire.
3. **Rose Locke** b.1526 - d.1613
   m. Anthony Hickman (d.1573) 28th Nov 1543 St. Mary-Le Bow, London
   Anthony was a Mercer of London and son of Walter of Woodford.

   1. Mary b. Jan 6th 1547
      m1. John Ansham or Amondesham of Ealing 1567.
      m2. Richard Phillips of Middlesex.
      a. Jerome Phillips B.D. (living in 1637).
      b. William Phillips, Lieutenant d.Breda, 1624/5
         m. Rose Rookwood of Norfolk and had two daughters.

25 .Directory of National Biography' Vol. 1-20.

c. Edward Phillips, Merchant, living in 1637 with sons.
d. Richard Phillips, Merchant, living in France in 1637.
e. Anne Phillips d.1628 –leaving six sons & a daughter- all living in 1637.
m. Walter Cary,Clerk.
f. Rose Phillips alive in 1637 with one surviving daughter – 4 sons deceased..
m. William Toll, Clerk, d.before 1637

2. William b. June16th 1549-d.1625
m1. Agnes Draper d. Feb 22nd 1600
m2. Elizabeth Willoughby b. - d.1622
a. Anne b. Oct 4th, 1601 - d. Sept.1602
b. Frances b. 31st, Oct 1602 - d.c1674
(m. William Rokeby 1624)
c. Willoughby b. 25th, May 1604 - d. 1649
d. William b. 18th May 1606 – d 3rd Sept. 1607
e. Thomas b. 21st, Feb 1607- d after 1625 Lawyer.
f. Mildred b. 11th, Oct 1610- 19th June 1628

3. Henry b. Dec 7 b 1550- d.1618 buried at Gainsborough.
m. Anne Wallop 8th April 1601.
a. Anthony b-d.1647
b. Elizabeth
m. Sir Henry Fynes (Fiennes) or Clinton (son of Henry, Earl of Lincoln)
c. Anne Hickman b.1604-d.1670
m. Richard Dukeson, Rector of St. Clement Danes.

4. Walter b. 26th Aug. b.1552 - d. Dec 29th, 1617
m. Elizabeth Staines of Essex, Nov 21st, 1586 at Ealing, Middlesex,
baptized 10th Dec 1567 St. Andrews, Holborn, London –
a. Dixie b. 8th Jan.1589 -d. Oct.10th 1631
m. Elizabeth Windsor, dau. of Sir William Windsor, 5th Lord.
Buried. Nov.2nd 1631 St. Mary Magdalene, Richmond.
b. Elizabeth m. George Alington of Swinhope at Gainsborough, 1617.
m. William Painter Esq.
c. William d. unmarried.
d. Walter d.1593- unmarried.
e. Anne Hickman- buried 19th Sept. 1598 at St. Mary Magdalene, Richmond, Surrey.

5. Unknown child born at 'Chilswell' Nr. Oxford c.1554/55

6. Unknown child born in Antwerp c.1557/58

7. Anthony b.Nov.17th, 1560- d. Dec 13th, 1597

8. Eleazer born before 1573-d. 1618.

9. Matthew born before 1573 – d. after 1637.
m. unknown
a. Frances
b. Mary
c. Rose

m2. Simon Throckmorton of Brampton after 1573.No issue.

4. **John Locke**, b.1527 .Went to Jerusalem in 1553, and Guinea in 1554 – d. in France 1558.

5. **Alice Locke** b.1528 d.1537

6. **Thomasin Locke** b. - d.1530

7. **Henry Locke** b.1536 d.1570-71
   m. Anne Vaughan b c 1530 –d c1621 9 definitely after 1616)-
      a) Anne died young in Geneva.
      b) Henry Locke the Poet, 3rd son b 1553?- d 1608?
         m. .Ann Moyle of Cornwall. Had two sons Henry b1592 and Charles.

8. **Michael Locke** b. around 1532 – d. around 1616 , of London, merchant;
   m1. Jayne Wilkinson.
      a) Zacharia
      b) Eleazar
      c) Gersom
      d) Benjamin
      e) William
      f) Anne m. Bleuett – Cornwall.
      g) Joan m Sansom
      h) Elizabeth.
   m2. Margery Peryn, Wid. of Caesar Dalmarias, MD of Venice (father of Sir Julius Caesar, Knight).

9. **Elizabeth Locke** b. Aug 3, 1535.
   m1. Richard Hill, Mercer of London (d.1568), had 13 children
   m2. Nicholas Bullingham, Bishop of Worcester.

10. **John Locke** b. Oct 13 1537-d. Oct 14th 1537.

The Locke DNA Project

American readers may be interested in the theory that Rose Hickman's great, great, great nephew, William Locke settled in Woburn, Massachusetts having sailed to America as a young boy. While in some quarters yet another of her descendants is purported to be John Locke the famous philosopher.

Below is the genealogy put forward by John Goodwin Locke in 'The Book Of Lockes' published in 1853 demonstrating that John Locke the Philosopher and William Locke of Woburn were first cousins.

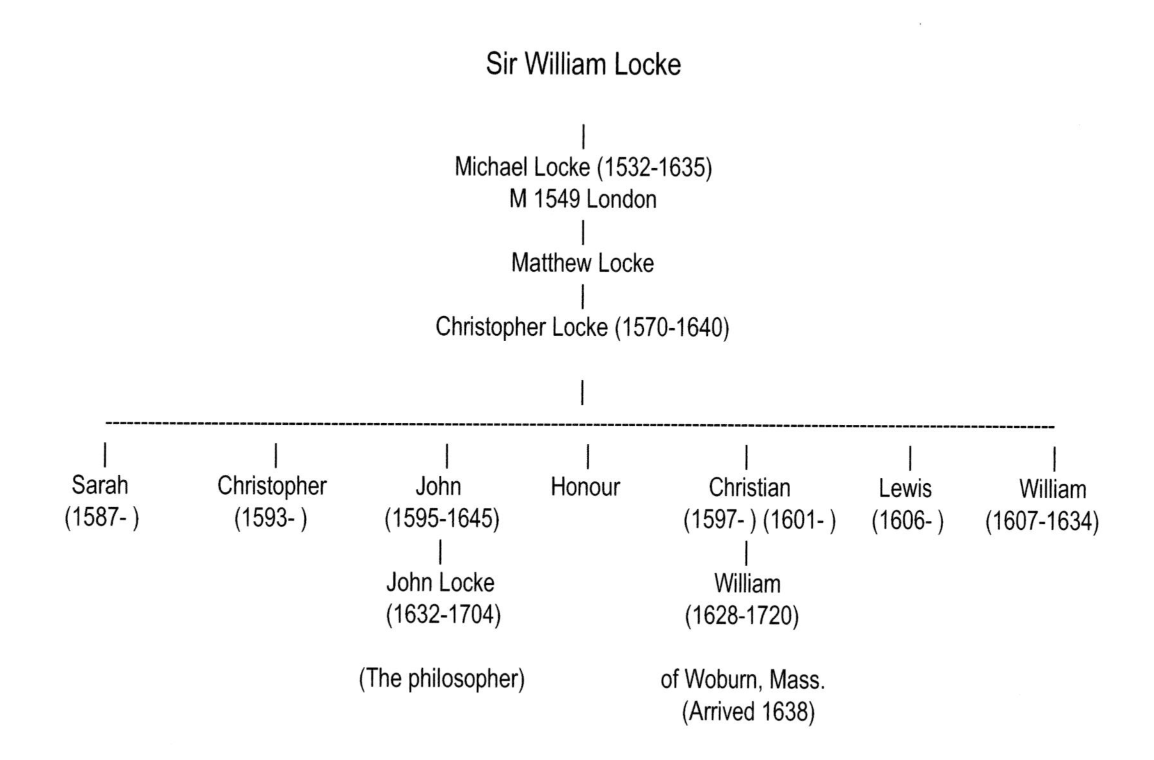

However, errors have been found elsewhere in this volume and, as at the time of writing, John Goodwin Locke's assumption cannot not be fully proved and substantiated by existing paper records. Hence widespread DNA testing amongst fully documented and partially proven lines may prove of immense value to family researchers.

The Locke DNA project was started in 2005. This project was started to try to connect the many Lock / Locke lineages of England and the USA. By comparing the male Y chromosome, we can tell which Locke branches are related, and which aren't.

Knowing which branches share the same Y chromosome, the family researchers can then focus their research specifically on the branches that are a DNA match to each other, in hopes of being able to connect the branches using the paper records.

The DNA project is in dire need of more Lock/Locke men from England to get involved in this project. With the help of our British Cousins, our trees may grow in a way that we could have never imagined. This project will be a benefit for both British and American Lock (e)'s alike. For more details visit www.lockeroots.home.comcast.net/~lockeroots/DNA1.html or contact Donald Locke, email address: lockeroots@comcast.net

References

'Notes to the diary: 1550-51', The Diary of Henry Machyn: Citizen and Merchant-Taylor of London (1550-1563)' (1848), pp. 313-323

'The Mercery of London: by Trade, Goods & People, and 1130-1578' by Ann F. Sutton

Calendar of State Papers from Henry VIII, Edward VI, Queen Mary and Queen Elizabeth.

'The Age of Drake' - James A. Williamson.

'English Voyages of Discovery' - Richard Hakluyt (various volumes).

'Histoire De Belgique 3rd Edition' - H. Pirenne

'The Baronetage of England' - Thomas Wotton, Edward Kimber, Richard Johnson

'The Travel Journal of Antonio de Beatis' - Edited by Hale and Lindon (The Hakluyt Society 1979)

'St. Mary The Virgin- A guide and History' by Lionel Green.

'Athenae Cantabrigienses' – Charles Henry Cooper, John Gray, Thompson Cooper.

'The Book of Lockes' - John Goodwin Locke (published 1853).

'Henry VIII (King and Court)' – A. Weir 1988

'Religion and Politics in mid-Tudor England through the eyes of an English Protestant Woman' by M Dowling and J Shakespeare, published in the 'Bulletin of the Institute of Historical Research, May 1982'.

'Cheapside: The central area', Old and New London: Volume 1 (1878).

'Lincolnshire Pedigrees' - Maddison, A.R (Ed.) 1902 Harleian Society.

Contemporary eye witness accounts written by various individuals 1525-1603

Lord King's *'Life of Locke'.*

My grateful thanks go to the following for their help and support in researching this book:

Roger Vorhauer.

Russell Hocking.

Dr. Jeremy Bangs.

Sir Nicholas Bacon, Bart.

Dr. Elizabeth Leedham-Green of Corpus Christi.

Gill Cannell of The Parker Library, Corpus Christi.

Lionel Green,

Teresa Cross, Parish Office, St. Mary Magdalene, Richmond.

Graham & Valerie Boyes.

David Agar of the Churches Conservation Trust (Wentworth Church).

Parish Office, St. Mary the Virgin, Merton.

And,

The History of Parliament Trust, London – unpublished article on Walter Hickman for 1604/29 section by Dr. Paul Hunneyball. I am grateful to the History of Parliament Trust for allowing me to see this article in draft.